By: Jim Golden

ISBN 978-0-557-17135-4

ADDITIONAL BOOKS BY JIM

Counterfeit Christianity vs. The Kingdom of God

PROPHECY: Search for the TRUTH

Significant Lives

What Is The GOSPEL of the KINGDOM?

Dedication

This small volume is dedicated to the Lord Jesus Christ. The reader should remember one basic yet deep truth as they read and that is that Jesus Christ is the true Gospel of God.

In Galatians Chapter two Paul makes this statement and I quote from The GOD's WORD translation, "But God, who appointed me before I was born and who called me by his kindness, was pleased to show me his Son. He did this so that I would tell people who are not Jewish that ***his Son is the Good News***. vv 15, 16.

His Son IS the GOOD NEWS! What a powerful truth. Everyting that follows is therefore designed to reveal Jesus to reader. It is not meant to give us a formula for successful Christian living, but rather to bring us to an end of life or living as we understand it so that we can actually become the clay vessels spoken of in the Scriptures that houses the Son of God. Christians are little Christs or Christ-bearers by actual definition of the word and that is what the Gospel (Good News) has come to accomplish.

Jesus, the WORD of God is revealed to us that he might then posses us and manifest his divine nature and life through us. AMEN! I encourage you to read this small volume with anticipation and faith. You are about to begin a journey into the depths of the ocean that is the life of Jesus—God's GOSPEL!

What is the Gospel?

Chapter 1
The Overview!

The word Gospel means good news. It is the kind of phrase that someone would use to make an announcement like, "I have good news, I just got a $3,000.00 a year raise, a company car with a gas allowance and a $1,700.00 per month expense account." So when God chose to make the announcement concerning his plan for creation he called it the Gospel—the good news!

It almost seems absurd to place God's Gospel in the same category as a company car or an expense account and in reality it is absurd because the core of the Gospel isn't just what it does for its followers. The Gospel is a person—JESUS IS the Gospel. Just how good this news is, is seldom realized or embraced by mankind until its truth becomes a living reality. These installments are designed to try and not only reveal the full impact of the good news of God, but to help make it a living reality in our lives. We do not just embrace a new religion, but the Son of God. We do not just enter into a new way of life, but into the life of

Christ! Salvation is not simply an individual mental belief that Jesus is the Son of God, but salvation belongs to him. Like the Gospel, salvation too is a person and we enter into it personally by entering into Jesus. Just how that is done, I pray, will be revealed in the following pages.

For just a moment let us go back in time approximately 2000 years to a small town in Judea, where the most incredible event ever conceived was getting ready to take place. The human race was about to be invaded by an alien life form. This life form was the only one of his kind. He had no recorded beginning, was absolutely omnipotent and existed outside of time and space. Months earlier he had implanted, in the ovulating human know as Mary, his seed, the seed of an uncreated indomitable life form. And now the time had finally come for her to birth this alien child. He would appear to be a human male child from all outward appearances, but the force of his life would be absolutely not of this world. He would become the progenitor of a new species of beings that had never before existed. While a special place of honor was reserved for him, he, never-the-less, was to be the prototype for a new race that he would birth. He would walk among these humans, share the frailty of their outward form, become fully acquainted with their pain and suffering, but he was not of this world.

This sounds almost like a science fiction novel, yet it is much closer to the true Gospel than the one we have heard preached for generations. Almost every Christian minister gives an invitation at the end of their message inviting anyone who wants, to come to Jesus and get saved, but what they are really saying is, "come to Jesus and get forgiven." I do not want to minimize forgiveness, I simply believe it is tragic that for many it ends there and we stop so short of what the sacrifice of Jesus is really meant to accomplish. It is partially the fear of being heretical that causes us to stop so short of proclaiming the full message of the Gospel. Do we dare proclaim that we are to be just like Jesus in every way? I am not merely speaking of imitation, but transformation.

The full Gospel answers so many unanswered questions. Questions like why can't we heal like Jesus did? Why do we seem so powerless to perform the "greater works" Jesus spoke of in John 14? Why are so many sick, diseased and even dyeing among the household of faith? Why aren't more coming to Christ? Why don't we love with the same intensity he did?

These are all valid questions that we, as "good" Christians, are often afraid to ask. Could it be that we don't really want to hear the answers? Yet many are beginning to muster the courage to ask them, even if it is under their breath out of pain or frustration. While I have by no means fully experienced the metamorphosis that Paul speaks of to the Corinthians, I have on occasion been allowed to enter this realm that Jesus lived in and I have seen the blind receive their sight and the dead raised to life. I am therefore compelled to write of these concerns in the hope that the Holy Spirit will begin to activate whatever truth there is in these writings within our lives.

While it may be difficult to overcome the indoctrinations of the past, with God all things are possible. Faith comes by hearing and hearing by the Word. How shall we be saved if we do not hear and how shall we hear if there is no preacher? Someone must take the risk of being ostracized or called a heretic to proclaim this Kingdom Gospel of metamorphosis continually until the transformation begins to overtake us.

This Pentecostal generation which was birthed when Peter stood and declared, "This is that which was spoken of by the prophet Joel," must live in the NOW of the Word as they did. We must embrace the true reason we were forgiven and what it really means to be made whole, today. Jesus said that his disciples were not of this world though they were in it. He often spoke metaphorically, but I believe this statement was more literal than metaphoric. The disciples lived a life of intense love and devotion just like him, talked like him and did the works that he did. Could it be that they had understood and embraced the deeper truth of the Gospel?

They didn't just stop at forgiveness or even being healed and delivered, but went on to be transformed into the alien children of God. We must be brutal in our assessments of our salvation experience and ask ourselves, "do I have Jesus or does Jesus have me?" The whole creation groans and travails to be delivered into the hands of these alien creatures—these sons and daughters of God. This is not a new doctrine it has always been in our Heavenly Father's heart. There is one out there who has done and will do everything he can to hinder the preaching of this Gospel, but he will not win. In fact, he has already lost, Hallelujah! We were forgiven and cleansed that we might be inhabited by this incredible life form we call God. And he is rewriting our DNA at the molecular level until anyone who is in Christ will truly become a NEW CREATURE!

It is important to note than when Jesus referred to the Gospel he also added, of the Kingdom. That was what the Gospel was going to produce. It was the Gospel of the Kingdom that had to be preached to the all nations and then the end would come. When he cast out demons with the finger of God then the Kingdom of God was in their midst. He spent his last forty days on earth after his resurrection revealing to them the Gospel of the Kingdom. Then after his ascension he sent them the Holy Spirit to continue to reveal to them the truth. The Spirit would take what was Jesus', and reveal it to them. I have often wondered what those days of instruction were like. I believe that what he was telling them they were becoming was so absolutely beyond their grasp that it took all of that time to awaken their hearts and minds to this amazing plan and work of God. I wonder how long it will take this generation to come into that reality?

What is the Gospel?

Chapter 2
The Progenitor!

In installment one we spoke of how an uncreated indomitable life form called God impregnated a human known as Mary with his seed and the male child she gave birth to became the progenitor of a new species. She named this child Jesus. From all outward appearances he was just like any other human but though he shared their outward appearance he was not of this world. The word progenitor is defined as originator: the originator of, or original model for, something. The Scripture declares that Jesus was the firstborn among many brothers and that he was the pattern son. This word pattern is the same word that is used for the pattern that women use to cut out material when they are making a garment so that it will be just like the original.

For a moment lets discuss a little of what Scripture reveals about Jesus—the progenitor. Hebrews declares that he is the brightness of God's glory and his express image. Jesus himself told his followers that he that had seen him had seen the Father. He said that he was in the Father and the Father was in him. He even went so far as to declare that he could not do anything unless the Father was doing it. It was more than just a dependant relationship or even a symbiotic one. Jesus was the Father clothed in an earth suit. It is a concept that my mind cannot understand fully from an intellectual point of view, but I can accept it by faith.

Now that we have established that Jesus and the Father were one then we can assume that one of his mission goals besides becoming the progenitor of a new species was to reveal what that species would be like by revealing the true and divine nature of his Father—God! In John 17 speaking with his Father in prayer he declared, " ... I have made Your name known to them, and will make it known, so that the love with which You loved Me may be in them, and I in them." NASB. It is of utmost importance to remember that God may have many unchangeable virtues like faithfulness, mercy, justice, righteousness, goodness and loyalty and on and on, but the very substance of which his uncreated being is made of is Love. The Scriptures declare that love is the only thing that cannot fail. I used to think that if God is love then love must be God, but that train of thought reduces an omnipotent uncreated being to an act and nothing is further from the truth. The fact that from time to time humans express "love" to one another can in no way be compared to this incomparable uncreated being.

This progenitor is therefore a being of love. It is this divine nature that determines every other aspect of his life. One of my favorite authors, A.W. Tozer, made a statement that went something like this, "What comes to your mind when you think about God is the most important thing about you." While it is impossible for a created limited being to even begin to grasp the concept of how utterly magnificent this God is, it behooves us to try. Tozer said, and I am paraphrasing, it is like trying to reach out and grab a star from the heavens. One will never succeed, but in reaching out we may point the way and at least gain a glimpse of him. It is impossible for us to personally rise above our conception of God or to realize the reality of his plan if we do not know either.

Another aspect of his love was revealed in his sacrificial death on the cross. No human ever suffered a more brutal and vile death than Jesus did. He was without fault and yet he bore all our sins in his own body on the tree so that he could extend to us his perfect forgiveness and righteousness. Scripture declares that it is our sin that has created a separation between us and our creator, but it also declares that for the joy set before him he endured the cross, despising the shame and sat down at the right hand of the throne of God. The reason that God doesn't distinguish between one sin and another is because sin creates within us a barrier of shame that hinders us from receiving of his love and salvation. God has always desired someone capable of returning his love and this new species alone can do that. We will discuss the ultimate plan of God—the Bride, in a later installment as well as just what this joy was and why this atonement was so absolutely necessary in order for him to complete his mission.

Suffice it to say that this altogether lovely one has won my heart and I can trust and follow this kind of God. He died for me when I was his enemy and hated his name. He did not say, "I will die for you if you will be good and do everything I tell you from now on," he just died. Isaiah said it like this, "He was wounded for our transgressions, he was bruised for our iniquities, the chastisement that brought us peace was placed upon him and by his wounds we were healed." The hymnist echoes this understanding when he says, "'twas there for sin which I have done he groaned upon the tree.

Amazing pity, grace unknown and love beyond degree." This is truly Good News! Somehow we tend to treat this as something to be accepted and then quickly moved on from to get to greater things. Gospel means good news and as Paul said in Romans, "I am not ashamed of the Gospel for it is the power of God for salvation..." If it is "the power" then there is no greater power it is THE POWER. Our understanding of the true and full Gospel is therefore paramount if we are to become this new species—the fruit of his resurrection.

What is the Gospel?

Chapter 3
How Do We Get There?

After my son read the first two installments he wrote me back the following response:

"Sounds good, now that I think about it I guess it all seems obvious to me, except how we go about getting there. Haven't people wanted this very thing since the beginning? What is your idea of what we need to do differently?"

My Response:

I think that one thing we need to do is to proclaim the transformation or metamorphosis more. I think another thing we need to do is to obey what Jesus said, "If any one would follow me, he must deny himself, take up his cross and follow me." The Gospel that we commonly hear preached centers around us, and our need for redemption not God's need or desire for a "counterpart" or "Bride".

The Gospel that he preached told us that we had to die on the cross along with him so that he could raise us up as a new species. Today's Gospel provides for our blessing and prosperity but speaks little of the fellowship of his sufferings, or coming to and end of our lives. While we retain that mystical aspect that makes us "us", the motivating and driving decision-making force in us should be his life.

Like Jesus said his works or words were not his own. I certainly don't have all the answers, but there is a growing hunger and cry in my life that doesn't want to continue on with business as usual. If Jesus came to create a new race of beings then I do not want to remain just a slightly better version of what I was. I wish I could wave a magic wand and see the revelation become a reality in my life. I am ashamed of how familiar I have become with the truth without actually fleshing it out. I heard someone say that familiarity often breeds contempt, and in a way that is true. We hear terms like "born again" so often that pretty soon they lose their meaning and impact. I think that a key to getting there is to first admit that we are not there and then to wait on God in faith and in expectation for what only he can do.

Jesus performed the miracle of changing water into wine in the beginning of his public ministry and the Scripture says that his disciples put their faith in him. As I understand it that's what it takes to be saved. Yet they still had a lot of issues like betrayal and denial. Then after his resurrection he breathed on them in the upper room and said to them, "receive the Holy Spirit." As far as I know he didn't fail and they received the Holy Spirit yet they still hid in fear of reprisal from the Jews and Romans. Then he commanded them to wait in Jerusalem until they received the ***Promise*** of the Father. He said that as a result of this encounter they would receive power and that they would become his witnesses. Well the word for power is what we get our English word for dynamite from and the word for witness is the Greek word *martos* that we get our English word martyr from. Most of us know what that is. Whatever happened after that encounter with the ***Promise*** of the Father changed them forever. Their love and devotion to Christ was so intensified that history records they seemed to be gripped by some holy madness. They did all the same miracles he did and these men, without the Internet, Television, Cable or any type of ad campaign turned the world upside down. And at the end of their lives their love, honor and devotion to Jesus only burned hotter and brighter as did their love for each other and the lost. Peter begged his executioners to crucify him upside down because he felt he was not worthy to die in the same manner as his precious Jesus did. Honestly, my heart does not burn with love for the church, the lost or Jesus in any measure close to theirs and I wonder what is wrong with this picture. It should, but selfishness and self indulgent self-centeredness still thrives in my life. Only rarely do I get a glimpse of what it should be like.

I know that I want what these men received and I don't believe I can get it from any study course, conference or tape series. I have actually been used by God to heal the blind and raise a man from the dead, but so did his disciples before their lives were changed forever. I am not certain what is going on in my life or in the lives of so many others that are saying, "I can no longer settle for anything less than what Jesus came to do to us!" I am certain that it is not just meant for us to lie around drunk in his Spirit, acting giddy and then the next day return to our same old lifestyles seldom even thinking of him in the course of the day. Don't get me wrong it is great to be in the "manifested" presence of God and it truly has an intoxicating effect on you, but I don't want to stop short and have that become the pursuit of my life. If I do, what has changed? My life is still all about me when it should be all about him. He came to clothe himself with flesh and blood 2000 years ago and he still wants to clothe himself in our humanity today. May God have mercy on this generation and once again send us the ***Promise*** of the Father that will change us forever into that new species of beings that never before existed until he came! Just for the sake of clarification I absolutely believe that the ***Promise*** is the person of Jesus Christ expressed in the person of the Holy Spirit.

What is the Gospel?

Chapter 4
The Work of the Cross!

For the preaching of the cross is to them that perish foolishness; but unto us which are saved it is the power of God. 1 Corinthians 1:18. It is verses like these that are seldom spoken of except around the time we celebrate the historic sacrifice of Jesus Christ. The cross was a road that Jesus declared he was destined to walk. He said in the garden of Gethsemane that for this purpose, his work on the cross, he came. Scripture also declares that Jesus was crucified before the foundations of the world, but revealed at just the right time. The cross was the place of ultimate triumph and victory, though for human eyes and demon eyes it looked quite the contrary. The utter despair that gripped his followers and his mother must have been devastating and overwhelming. His disciples had pinned all their hopes of Israel's deliverance on this "Messiah" who now hung dyeing on a tree. It was the kind of death that brought with it a curse and great dishonor, for it is written cursed is everyone who hangs on a tree.

But what the human eye couldn't discern nor the demonic world comprehend was that in his suffering and death he was gathering into himself every life that had ever lived. He was making a show openly of the powers and principalities, taking the handwriting of ordinances that was against us and nailing them to his cross. All of mankind died in him that day and as a result was set free from the judgment of the law by his righteous and holy blood. The Scripture declares that it was his own blood that brought him back from the dead!

To the intellectual mind this bloody religion is not only foolish, but absolutely barbaric, yet we seldom diminish the blood that was shed by our troops in all the wars they've fought in to gain our independence and keep the United States a free republic. How can the work that Jesus performed on the cross for the entire human race deserve any less respect, honor and praise? We need only put our trust in him.

One of the aspects I want to look at concerning the work of the cross and how it changed my life was the role of personalization. It is not enough for us to admit that Jesus died on the cross as an historical fact. While that is true we must come to the realization that he died on that cross for each one of us personally. Then we must take a step further enter into a complete and absolute identification with him. I believe that one reason the Scripture records the story of the thieves that died with Jesus on his right and left was to give us a picture of the choice that was set before us. We cannot just come to Jesus with an intellectual acknowledgement of what he did. This type of belief won't do it. The Scripture says that we believe in one God and we do well, the demons believe also and tremble. A very sobering fact. Jesus actually made it very difficult to follow him. When he said, "if any man would follow me he must deny himself, take up his cross and follow me." I can guarantee that he wasn't on his way to a fine dinner, but to a horrific death.

While we may never suffer the same brutal vilifying death that he did, he never-the-less is asking us to come to an end of our lives as we know them to be his witnesses. Narrow is the gate that leads to life and few they are that find it. God is patient, not willing that any should perish, but that all should come to repentance, but he will not always strive with mankind. I am not trying to scare anyone into being a "better" Christian or to put more money into the offering plate, but to help us to realize that if we want what Jesus wants and came to give us then we too must let the cross have its perfect work in our lives.

Nothing should be more important than learning to hear his voice and obey him instantly. To obey is better than sacrifice. I have often wondered exactly what that means. Over three decades as a "Christian" I have begun to open my eyes a little. The obedience part comes when we realize that Jesus came to do more than just forgive us. He has a plan to actually transform us into a species of being that never before existed until his death and resurrection. Our acknowledgment and pursuit of this can be the obedient goal of our lives. He commanded the disciples to wait in Jerusalem until they received the Promise of the Father. Will we obey the same command and wait until we receive the Promise?

The sacrifice comes when we stop short of this full Gospel and wallow in the pool of forgiveness only believing ourselves to be hopeless sinners destined to fail over and over again until one day the chariot of God will come for us and we will go to a far better place. Yes, I believe that we will all one day dwell in a new heaven and earth wherein righteousness dwells, but I also believe that we can and should on a daily basis experience days of heaven on earth. John said that he saw the Holy city, the new Jerusalem descending out of Heaven as a Bride adorned for her husband. I do not think he was speaking only of some future point in time, but of those truly born from above in every generation here and now.

One of the tendencies of the prophetic gift is to continually put things into the future, but the true prophetic anointing has within it not only the ability to foretell events, but to pronounce the present reality of the prophetic and written word of God being fulfilled in our midst.

I am not altogether certain how we can crucify ourselves with Christ. It is impossible to nail our own hands to a cross, but with God all things are possible and I want to be more than metaphorically crucified with my Jesus Christ, that I may also be raised with him in newness of life not just in the age to come, but in the here and now!

What is the Gospel?

Chapter 5
The Master Plan, The Bride!

Sometime ago I read a book for the second time by a man named Gene Edwards called, THE DIVINE ROMANCE. Normally this kind of book is not my cup of tea, (being the "Rambo" type), but the truth of the story line so gripped my heart that it actually changed the way I thought of God, his plan and his purpose for creation. Imagine for a moment that there is no universe. Time and space doesn't exist yet there is only this alien being. I use the word alien because in many ways he is so absolutely different from us. Everything that exists or that does not yet exist, exists within him. He is alone, the only one of his kind, the only one of any kind. Yet within the very substance of this being's composition is an unquenchable burning fire. A fire so intensely passionate, so intensely hot that all the suns in all the galaxies that we have come to know over our short existence couldn't even come close to its heat. Throughout the millennia, we have come to define this essence as LOVE. Love, the most powerful force in all of creation.. This alien being of Love we have come to know as GOD!

As a Christian we are taught that God is absolutely complete within himself, lacking nothing. For God to be lacking anything would make him incomplete and the very thought of God being incomplete would be considered sacrilege. Yet the very concept of love has within it the need to give. This is not what I consider a negative, but as positive a positive as you can have. I believe that from what we humans call the beginning it has always been God's desire to have a helpmeet. It is evident in his entire creation. For every corporeal life form there is a male and a female of the species. I do not know that much about the angelic world, but I believe, as some do, that there are no two alike and that they were not created in God's image. However, when it came to the creation of man the Scripture declares that God created man in his image. Obviously there is one major difference that can never be bridged and that is that we are created while God is uncreated. He has no beginning of days and no ending of days. He is way beyond a creature that has eternal life and everything that exists, exists within him.

What then are the characteristics that make us, alone among his creation, like him? We have the ability to freely give love without asking anything in return. We can experience the full range of emotions. We are basically a spiritual being, with a soul in a body. In God's great plan to have his soul-mate, counterpart or bride he had to devise a plan that even his enemies couldn't understand or thwart! So he created the human species and gave them the greatest gift of all—free will. But what is free will without any choices to make? So entered Satan, the tempter, the great deceiver, unwittingly a tool in God's hand to accomplish his ultimate intention. I have often wondered what the first man, Adam, was like before he ever made his choice to go after the knowledge of good and evil instead of continuing on in an ever deepening relationship with God. He must have been awesome. The truth of the matter is that it was necessary for this race of humans to fall from their first estate in order for them to evolve into a race of beings that could actually choose, with the full knowledge of all their options, God's way. Paul speaks a lot about this unique, one-flesh relationship shared in the holy state of matrimony. Its level of intimacy between the bride and groom is unique among all other covenant relationships in the Word, but is actually a metaphoric view of Jesus and his Bride.

When Jesus came along it was the perfect timing of God. Once God actually became the sacrifice for the sin that separated mankind from God he could then redeem mankind from the influence of the tempter and bring them into a place of eternal security. Once that was accomplished through his work on the cross, then this God, who clothed himself in humanity to become the progenitor of a new species, could, after his resurrection from the dead, send his own uncreated Spirit into the lives that he had purchased with his own precious blood. This act would eventually create a race of men and women that had never before walked upon planet earth. Jesus was the first one of this race, but he would not be the last. Now that his plan was successful he would give birth to a whole race of people just like him. People who, though they lived in this world, were not of this world and it would be evident by their love and the power they wielded.

Though this race would span thousands of years and hundreds of cultures, they would share one thing that would forever bind them together irrevocably, God's uncreated eternal Spirit—The Holy Spirit. This is one of the most powerful truths in Scripture. The Word says that when one member rejoices we all rejoice and when one suffers we all suffer. Because we live out our lives in these isolated biological forms we call "bodies" we have adopted the idea that we are somehow not truly a part of each other, but in reality nothing could be further from the truth. That is what God has been trying to reveal to us for thousands of years. If we ever truly grasp the impact of this we will see the face of the Church changed overnight and the Bride will have made herself ready. I am at a loss for words to declare what this Bride means to her lover Jesus, but I know that it is only the Spirit and the Bride that have the ability to call Jesus down from the heavens – for it is the Spirit and the Bride that say COME!

What is the Gospel?

Chapter 6
The Appointed Time, The Harvest!

When I was writing these installments they were preceded by a very powerful dream that I had. The theme or repeating phrase in the dream was, "You have to do what you have to do to be what you have to be, for you were created to be a son of God, wielding all the power of the age to come!" There was much more to this dream, but in it I questioned the one who was explaining different aspects of the dream to me. I assume this person was God or at least one of his delegated representatives. I said to this person, "men have understood and taught this before. What makes this time any different?" The answer came back simply, "The Appointed Time of the Lord!"

This was not the first time that particular phrase has caught my attention. Once I had a vision of a valley surrounded by huge mountains. At one end the valley was closed by a gigantic dam that went all the way to the top of two of the highest mountains. They were like doorposts for this dam. Below in what was nearly a dry riverbed people played in little puddles of water that had been created by small little holes in the wall of this dam. As I looked closer I saw several of these holes had corresponding pools of water with people gathered around their particular puddle playing in the water.

They didn't seem to be too aware of each other, but my attention was drawn to the small holes in the dam that had or were still feeding these little pools of water. Over each one was a name, like Azusa Street, Welsh Revival, or Pentecost, etc. At the very top of the vision over the dam there were the most ominous storm clouds thick with rain and full of lightning and thunder. I noticed a crack that was starting to open in the middle of the dam and the water level was already so high it could be seen from my lower vantage point. I knew that this was going to break and that no force could stop it. Then a sign appeared by this crack like the signs near the other little holes. It read, "The Appointed Time of the Lord!"

As all these things ran through my mind God began to speak to me about his Gospel being the key to the fulfillment of these and other visions and dreams I have had over the last 33 years. Scriptures like, "I am not ashamed of the Gospel for it is the power of God", the special relationship revealed about Christ and the Church and the revelation about the metamorphosis that the born again go through by the renewal of their mind coupled with all of the references of Jesus' metaphoric or not so metaphoric statements began to be woven together like some beautiful tapestry that was so intricate and yet so simple it compelled me to write book.

Imagine with me about this time when the creation's groaning and travailing finally delivers it into the hands of these sons and daughters of God. Jesus was just one man, the progenitor, the prototype, and the pattern son for a whole new species of beings. No wonder he was able to make statements like he did when he said, "the works that I have been doing you shall do also and even greater works than these shall you do." He wasn't fantasizing, or daydreaming, but seeing the revelation that had burned in his Father's heart, before there was ever time or eternity, coming to pass.

Did you ever wonder why, when from all outward appearances it looked like harvest time was still four months away, Jesus could say to his disciples that the fields were already white for harvest? He told them to pray to the Lord of the Harvest for more laborers and yet the Lord of the Harvest was standing right there beside them. I think that he wanted them to realize that he, not natural circumstances or appearances, determined the when and where of harvest time. Jesus is the Lord of the Harvest and he wants people to see from his perspective and ask for the resources we need to bring in the harvest.

I sometimes like to imagine what it was like to walk down those dusty roads with Jesus. Stopping by a well and seeing him heal a blind man and then telling a woman of questionable character everything about her or granting the request for the healing of a soldier's child with such authority that from that very moment many miles away the child was made well. Or having to say the name Lazarus come forth so that every one that was dead would not rise to life. Who of us, at one time or another, hasn't said, "If Jesus were only here things would be different?" Yet that is the whole point of his Master plan—to create us in his image! If we spent a little more time meditating on and declaring these revelations to each other and ourselves we might just begin to see revelation turned into reality. I used to think that revelation was the end of it, after all it is the name of the last book in our Bible, but I have learned that, like knowledge, if revelation doesn't become reality it can only puff you up and make you think you are something that you are not. Knowledge/revelation puffs up but love edifies. With such revelation our greatest concern should be how it can become a living reality in our lives.

The Appointed Time!

Above is an image of the vision I had that is referenced in this chapter. I created it using an imaging software. However, I was unable to adequately capture the powerful impact the actual vision had upon me. I was left breathless by the impending and sudden nature of the event.

What is the Gospel?

Chapter 7
The Blink of an Eye!

In writing these installments I want to stress emphatically that my purpose is in no way to bring Christ down from his place of absolute God, and Redeemer. Jesus will forever be completely unique. He is by definition, "life"—uncreated God and we are his redeemed. My intention is to exalt to the place it deserves the perfect work he accomplished through the Gospel. Besides the fact that he has done all that he has done for us freely, he has also, as a part of the Gospel package, made us his ministers of reconciliation. Think about how incredible that concept is. In order for us to do what he did we have to be like he was in this world. Scripture says, "it does not yet appear what we shall be, but we know that when he appears we shall be like him for we shall see him as he is." (1John 3:2). A popular song declares over and over the phrase, "in a moment, in the blink of an eye that's why I'm alive for the blink of an eye."

The Gospel of Jesus Christ is something that we need to declare to one another and ourselves each day until we actually change through the incredible grace that resides it its truth. I am talking about thinking about this incredible good news everyday until we go through a metamorphosis that will turn us into his ministers of reconciliation. The thought of being reconciled to God is staggering by itself, but then for that reconciliation to have with it so much trust and honor that he would actually make us his ministers of reconciliation goes beyond my ability to understand and embrace the magnitude of that kind of love.

The Gospel is declaring, that not only are we not pond scum, we are of such incredible value that God would brutally sacrifice his only Son for us that he may love us with the same love that He and Jesus shared. But it doesn't stop there, he then goes on to say not only do I love you this much, but because love by its very nature must give itself away to someone else, I am entrusting you all with the ministry of reconciliation. Wait a minute, that's not the end of it. In order that you will have guaranteed success, and bear much remaining fruit, I will give you everything you need to accomplish this—my very own life shall come and dwell in you.

This is not just a figure of speech, a beautiful thought to be shared at Easter time, or a grand illusion, but a living reality that has burned in God's heart before the beginning of time. For us to be his helpmeet, the very Bride of Jesus Christ standing beside him without shame or inferiority now and in the age to come, is the passionate desire not only of his heart, but of every Christian who has laid hold on the understanding of the Gospel. Oh what good news this is! It is definitely not something to be looked at as "religion 101" and then moved on from, but should be the main and daily pursuit of our existence.

In conclusion I only wish you could feel the pain and passion that burns in my heart as I write these words. It is impossible for pen and paper, the tongues of men or angels or anything in all of creation to adequately express the glorious love and grace of our God, which he extended to us through Jesus Christ. We are not some creative whim of a bored omnipotent creative force. We were the reason for his creation. I cannot love a worm like I can love my wife and on the evolutionary scale that is what we as natural beings are compared to God. But, the good news is that with God all things are possible and because of his great love with which he has loved us he has allowed us to actually partake of His divine nature. (2 Peter 1:4).

Just what does that mean? To actually house within these clay vessels such unimaginable glorious treasure should take our breath away. Maybe that is why I have seen so many people pass out on the floor, overcome by the glory of God. Their minds cannot comprehend what his Spirit and divine nature are doing, but you can be certain, he is at work within us both to will and to work his good pleasure. I personally think that the Mount of transfiguration was not just God showing off or trying to amaze us, but a taste of things to come.

I believe as the transforming power of the Gospel grows in its manifested strength in the days ahead in preparation for the greatest harvest the world has ever seen, that the glory hidden in these jars of clay will from time to time not be able to retain or conceal him who has become our life. Remember to keep your lamps full. Remember as well that the oil in that lamp has a purpose and that is to burn. To burn so brightly that it gives light to all around it. "Burn in me", as the song says, "Burn in me, let the fire of the Holy One burn in me." We all share the same Spirit, the same life and we all have one Father and God of all, so let us embrace love and forgiveness that when Jesus returns he will find faith on the earth—for faith works through love! No matter what one day corruption will put on incorruption and mortality will put on immortality—in the blink of an eye!

www.ingramcontent.com/pod-product-compliance
Ingram Content Group UK Ltd.
Pitfield, Milton Keynes, MK11 3LW, UK
UKHW020229250726
13967UKWH00001B/275

9 780557 171354